KENNY ROGERS

THROUGH THE YEARS

COUNTRY MUSIC HALL OF FAME AND MUSEUM NASHVILLE

HONOR THY MUSIC®

COUNTRY MUSIC FOUNDATION PRESS

222 Fifth Avenue South • Nashville, Tennessee 37203

(615) 416-2001

978-0-915608-23-2

This publication was created by the staff of the Country Music Hall of Fame® and Museum.

Editors: Mick Buck and John W. Rumble

Printer: Lithographics, Inc., Nashville, TN

Except where otherwise credited, images in this book come from the collection of the Country Music Hall of Fame® and Museum.

CONTENTS

Award presented to Rogers by the National Cowboy Hall of Fame and Western Heritage Center for his role as host and narrator of the 1993 documentary *The Real West.*
Courtesy of Kenny Rogers / Photo by Bob Delevante

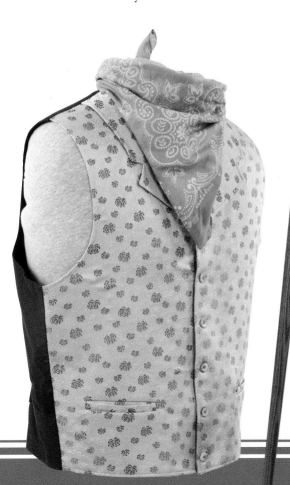

Rogers's clothing and props for the 1980 TV movie *Kenny Rogers As The Gambler* included this vest, bandana, and cane.
Courtesy of Kenny Rogers / Photo by Bob Delevante

KENNY ROGERS
THROUGH THE YEARS

In a career spanning more than fifty years, Kenny Rogers has left an indelible mark on American music. As a singer, he has used his trademark husky voice to record thirty-six Top Ten country records, including twenty-one #1 hits. Many of these have crossed over into other musical fields, enlarging country's audience in the process. As of 2014 he has sold more than 120 million albums worldwide. One of the first country artists to fill large arenas, his stage shows continue to draw large crowds.

In addition, his broad musical tastes, diverse talents and interests, strong work ethic, and relentless quest for perfection have made him a successful actor, photographer, author, and playwright.

Brass belt buckle, late 1970s.
Courtesy of Ron Harman / Photo by Bob Delevante

HONOR THY MUSIC®

August 13, 2014

Dear Museum Friend,

Born August 21, 1938, in Houston, Kenny Rogers grew up in one of the most impoverished areas of the city. His inspiring path to superstardom began on his grandfather's porch, where his very musical family often gathered to play, and where he first heard live music.

Kenny soon realized that music and a strong penchant for storytelling songs were in his genes. In high school, he sang with a vocal harmony group that primarily covered radio hits of the day. In the early 1960s he played bass and sang in a jazz outfit, and at mid-decade he joined folk-pop group the New Christy Minstrels. Eventually, ex-members of the Minstrels formed the First Edition, which became Kenny Rogers and the First Edition.

Kenny Rogers and the First Edition's "Ruby, Don't Take Your Love to Town," exploded in 1969 as both a pop and country hit, and it endures today as one of the most moving and powerful singles ever recorded. "Ruby" became the template for the kind of modern, socially conscious musical tale that would win Kenny a lifetime of hits as a solo artist. Though he had songs that made both the country and pop charts, Kenny found his permanent home in country music.

In 1986, the museum opened *Kenny Rogers' America: Sights and Insights*, an exhibition of thirty-five black-and-white photographs taken by the singer on his far-ranging concert tours. In the same year, for his dedication to humanitarian causes, Kenny received the first Roy Acuff Award, sponsored by the *Tennessean*, the Gannett Foundation, and the Country Music Hall of Fame and Museum.

In 2012, as the museum's artist-in-residence, Kenny presented two evenings of unique, intimate performances in our Ford Theater. The following year, reflecting his many contributions to the popularity of country music, Kenny was elected to the Country Music Hall of Fame.

We now welcome you to *Kenny Rogers: Through the Years*, an exhibit that provides a snapshot of his extended and richly varied career. I know that you'll enjoy exploring Kenny's musical accomplishments and his achievements as actor, photographer, and champion of humanitarian endeavors.

Sincerely,

Kyle Young, Director
Country Music Hall of Fame® and Museum

FOREWORD

Kenny is one the great loves of my life. Yes, I said it. I love Kenny Rogers.

I've loved his music from the start, back in 1967, when he was part of that great group the First Edition. He did one of my favorite songs ever, "I Just Dropped In (To See What Condition My Condition Was In)." Then I met Kenny personally when he was kind enough to do my very first *Dolly* TV show back in the '70s. We've worked many shows together since that time, and my love for Kenny has only grown through the years.

No, we have never been involved romantically, but we share a great love and passion for each other. Our hearts and our souls connect and certainly our music does, too. We make each other happy. And to be happy in a relationship is a sure way to have it last forever.

Kenny is one of the greatest men I've ever known. He is smart, kind, well mannered, a real gentleman, and very handsome. He is a man's man and a woman's fantasy. He has a great ear for great songs, and he has chosen some of the greatest songs of all time. He has written or co-written many of them and has suggested the ideas and worked on many that he does not even take credit for. He knows his music and he knows what he wants.

Finding and knowing a great song truly is a gift, but Kenny has many gifts. He has the gift of making people feel comfortable in his presence, whether he's on stage in front of thousands of people or just one-on-one in the dressing room or in the alley behind the Ryman or at a barbecue with friends and family. Everybody loves Kenny; he's good company.

Kenny has the gift of making people feel special . . . the gift of conversation, the gift of good humor, good taste, and good times. But the greatest gift that God ever gave him is that incredible voice. I never get tired of hearing him sing. He is a true stylist. I always feel every emotion I own when I hear Kenny sing. And he owns a song like nobody else I've ever known. I also love his speaking voice. I've loved hearing him do voice-overs on many different shows. He could make a living at that alone.

Oh, and did I mention he has a gift for photography? He is one of the greatest photographers I have ever seen and has photographed some of the biggest stars ever. The way he captures nature is incredible. So if you don't have any of his books on photography, you should get them. They're beautiful on your coffee table, and they're beautiful to look at, as well.

Kenny is a great family man, a great friend, and a great duet partner. It was my lucky day back in 1983 when Kenny and Barry Gibb called me to sing on "Islands in the Stream." It's been a great ride ever since. We were meant to be together. I believe that with all my heart. And I believe we always will be, whether in real life or in memories, and certainly through our music. I wouldn't have missed the chance to know Kenny Rogers.

To quote one of my favorite songs I've ever done with Kenny, "You can't make old friends." So, old friend, just know how much you are respected, admired, and appreciated, not only by me, but by millions of people all over the world. And just know that, through the years, I will always love you.

Dolly

THANK YOU

With a career that has spanned more than fifty-five years, it would be hard to thank everyone who had something to do with my success without inadvertently leaving someone out. So, to everyone involved in my endeavors, starting with the Bobby Doyle Three, through the First Edition, to the transformation to Kenny Rogers, solo artist—and YOU know who YOU are!—my heartfelt "THANK YOU" for all your support, guidance, and friendship through the years. Coming from the projects in Houston, Texas, I never dreamed that my career would take me to so many places. From photography to acting in movies and on the stage, I have been blessed to be surrounded by so many talented people who have guided me in all the right directions. Special thanks to Ken Kragen, Jim Mazza, and Ken Levitan—my managers from then to now!

Kyle Young and the entire staff at the Country Music Hall of Fame® and Museum, I am honored to be featured in an exhibit and I truly THANK YOU!

This exhibit is very special to me, as it portrays highlights from throughout my career. Carolyn Tate, your dedication, time, and effort to assemble the story are very much appreciated. Gene Roy, your foresight in saving my stage clothing, pictures, scripts, set pieces, and memorabilia has proved to be invaluable. Debbie Cross and Kirt Webster, you both traveled many miles and spent countless hours making sure that so many key items are part of this exhibit, and your contributions are also greatly appreciated.

THE KENNY ROGERS TEAM:

Vector Management
Ken Levitan
Bob Burwell
Jason Henke

William Morris Endeavor
Greg Oswald

Smith Wiles & Co.
Dwight Wiles
Kevin Dalton

Webster & Associates Public Relations
Kirt Webster
Jeremy Westby

SKH Music
Keith Hagan

Bruce Phillips Law
Bruce Phillips

Bloodline: The Band
Steve Glassmeyer
Randy Dorman
Chuck Jacobs
Warren Hartman
Gene Sisk
Brian Franklin
Mike Zimmerman

Kenny Rogers Productions Staff:
Gene Roy • *Tour Manager*
Debbie Cross • *Operations Manager*
Keith Bugos • *Production Manager*
Kelly Junkermann • *Creative Director*
Frank Farrell • *Technical Director*
Jeff Metter • *Lighting Director*
Eron Roy • *Audio Tech*
Tim Miller • *Backline*
Todd Honaker • *Special Effects/Set*
Doug Simpson • *Kenny's Bus Driver*
Harry McClure • *Band Bus Driver*
Danny McClure • *Truck Driver*

Kenny Rogers, 2013.
Courtesy of Kenny Rogers / Photo by Piper Ferguson

Bruce Mosier and Kenny Rogers of the Scholars, c. 1956.

Courtesy of Kenny Rogers

Detail of jacket worn by Kenny Rogers.

Courtesy of Kenny Rogers / Photo by Bob Delevante

MUSIC MAN

ROOTS

Since the late 1950s, Kenny Rogers has distinguished himself in many musical styles, from R&B, doo-wop, jazz, and folk to pop, country, and rock. Although he is best known for country story songs and smooth, country-pop love songs, he also has a deeply rooted stringband heritage.

The son of Lucille Rogers, a nursing assistant, and Floyd Rogers, a carpenter, Kenny was born in Houston in 1938, the fourth of eight children who lived with their parents in a public housing project. Floyd played fiddle and enjoyed making music with his guitar-playing brothers at family gatherings on Grandpa Byrd Rogers's farm in East Texas.

"As early as grade school," Kenny recalled, "I began to see music and singing as a respite from all the awkwardness and embarrassment of growing up poor, shy, and often an outsider."

Above: Rogers was named Most Talented in Jefferson Davis High School's 1956 yearbook.
Courtesy of Sharman Pirkle and Susan Bradley

Right: Rogers, age seventeen.
Courtesy of Kenny Rogers

senior

MOST TALENTED
Kenneth Rogers
Don Angelo
Jim Blasdell

Left: Nineteen-year-old Kenny Rogers at the time he appeared on *American Bandstand*, 1957.
Courtesy of Kenny Rogers

Below: Rogers portrayed Mr. Wilson, the high school principal, in his senior class production of the popular Broadway comedy *Time Out for Ginger*.
Courtesy of Kenny Rogers

"Time Out For Ginger"

A comedy in three acts
by
RONALD ALEXANDER

CAST

Lizzie, the maid .... LUDA KARNAUGH
Agnes Carol .... MOLLY GREER
Howard Carol .... JIM BLASEDELL
Joan, their daughter, age 18 .... LINDA GLASS
Jeannie, their daughter, age 16 .... CAROLYN PATTERSON
Ginger, their daughter, age 14 .... PAT COUSINS
.... CONNIE GUNNELS
Eddie Davis .... LUTHER DAVIS
Tommy Green, Ginger's boyfriend .... JERRY PENNICK
Mr. Wilson, high school principal .... KENNETH ROGERS
Priscilla Jones, private secretary, to bank
  president .... SHARON MERCHANT

Synopsis of Scenes

ACT I

The living room of the home of Mr. and Mrs. Howard Carol. Early Fall, 4:30 one afternoon.

ACT II

Scene I Four weeks later
Scene II A Saturday afternoon, four weeks later.

ACT III

The same afternoon.

PRODUCTION STAFF

Student Director .... SHELBY HAVENS
Script Girl—Technical Director .... LINDA HOLDER
Business Manager .... TENNEY GRIFFIN
House Manager .... VALMA VALLE
Programs .... ROBERT SHELBY
  Cover (design) .... ERNEST GARCIA
Tickets .... JANELLE WIGGINS
  Design .... MANUEL VALLE
Lobby .... BARBARA RUSSELL
  Concessions .... LANELL WOFFARD
Head Usher .... DOLORES WOMACK
Stage Manager .... JESSE MENDOZA
Publicity .... DORAL SKAINS, PAT FERGERSON
Props .... LOIS GREMPSZYNSKI
Make-up .... JANICE JOHONNESSON
Costumes .... LOIS GERMPSZYNSKI
Electrician .... GENE MCCARTY
Special Effects .... ROY CASTELLO
Doorman .... RICHARD LAWSON
Inter Communication .... RUDY CASTILLA
Music .... SAMMY GARCIA
Art .... DAVID RODGERS

Our Appreciation to Faculty Advisors

Passes, etc. .... OFFICE STAFF AND ADMINISTRATION
Art .... CARL HAYES
Beauty Hints .... DOTTIE LEE
Typing .... OPAL HATCHER
Music .... M. H. MCNEELY
Mimeograph .... MINNIE SAHUALLA
Lobby .... ANITA SMITH
Special Effects .... Ex Student—ED THIELANN

Also

PAUL'S T. V. SERVICE
NORTH SIDE TRANSFER AND STORAGE CO.
HOME FURNITURE AND APPLIANCE CO.

This page:

Right: The Scholars, c. 1957. Clockwise, from top right: Bruce Mosier, Kenny Rogers, Al Eisemann, Perry McClendon, unidentified.
Courtesy of Kenny Rogers

Below: Between 1956 and 1957, the Scholars recorded four singles distributed nationally by Dot and Imperial.
Courtesy of Sharman Pirkle and Susan Bradley

Facing page: (clockwise, from top right):

The Scholars, 1956.
Clockwise from left: Bruce Mosier, Kenny Rogers, Cody Garner, Don Angelo.
Courtesy of Kenny Rogers

Rogers's first solo single, "That Crazy Feeling," released in 1957.
Courtesy of Sharman Pirkle and Susan Bradley

The Scholars, c. 1957.
Courtesy of Kenny Rogers

THE SCHOLARS

Working part-time jobs, Rogers bought a Gibson "Eddy Arnold" guitar on the installment plan. During 1956 and 1957, he sang with fellow high school students in a vocal act, the Scholars. The group often sang doo-wop and R&B numbers they heard on the radio. "Although I played the guitar," Rogers explained, "we were primarily a vocal group. . .We were in high demand, or so we thought. Performing for free added a lot of luster to our career."

The act recorded for Cue, Imperial, and Dot Records. Rogers's solo recording of "That Crazy Feeling" became a hit for the New York-based Carlton label. Performing on a local television program helped him snag an appearance on Dick Clark's popular ABC-TV show *American Bandstand*.

"KENNY IS SUCH A GREAT SINGER"

"Kenny is such a great singer. He has complete control of his throat, especially the tremolo, or vibrato, in his voice, which he can make as rapid or as slow as he wants. When I was engineering his sessions for Larry Butler, his producer at United Artists, Kenny recorded most of his vocals all the way through. Sometimes he'd re-record small parts of a vocal if he or Larry weren't totally satisfied, and I'd blend those parts into the vocal track. But Kenny didn't have to do that very much; with a lot of artists, it wasn't that way. Kenny was that good—just an *excellent* singer.

"Also, he can make you believe he's really into the song, whether he is or not. The majority of the time, he was. But even if Kenny was really tired—I've even seen him out there at the microphone yawning—he has the ability to make you believe he's feeling the song all the way. Very few singers can do that as well as he can.

"And Kenny has that 'growl' in his voice that's so effective. I remember one time he asked Larry, 'Am I growling too much?'

"Larry said, 'If you're not growling, we ain't makin' no money!'"

—studio engineer Billy Sherrill

Facing page: Rogers's self-titled second album for United Artists Records, released in 1977, was produced by Larry Butler and engineered by Billy Sherrill and Harold Lee.

UA-LA689-G
JAMARG, Inc.

THE BOBBY DOYLE THREE

Next, Rogers joined a Houston-based jazz trio led by piano player Bobby Doyle. Doyle put the young musician on stand-up bass and vocals, and Rogers proved a quick study as Doyle led the act in seemingly endless rehearsals. Rogers later identified Doyle as "the best musician I had ever worked with."

Doyle's trio teamed with Kirby Stone's band to work concerts and clubs across the nation. "We played a lot and learned a lot about harmony, arrangement, and stage performance," Rogers said. "I carried all of these things with me as I later moved from genre to genre."

Right: The Bobby Doyle Three. Top to bottom: Kenny Rogers, Don Russell, Bobby Doyle. *Courtesy of Kenny Rogers*

Below: Kenny Rogers's brother Lelan produced this single by the Bobby Doyle Three for Houston's Towne House label, c. 1962. *Courtesy of Sharman Pirkle and Susan Bradley*

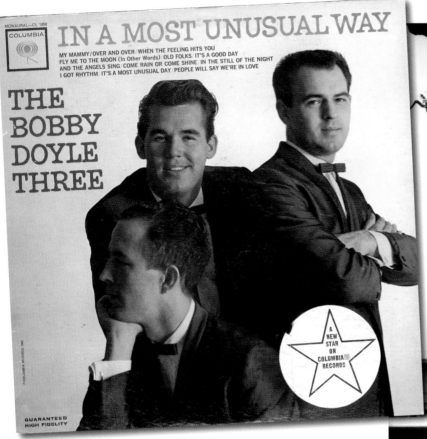

Above left: The Bobby Doyle Three's LP, *In a Most Unusual Way*, released in 1962. *Courtesy of Sharman Pirkle and Susan Bradley*

Above: Don Russell, Bobby Doyle, Kenny Rogers. *Courtesy of Kenny Rogers*

Left: Bobby Doyle, Don Russell, Kenny Rogers of the Bobby Doyle Three, at the release party for Rogers's album *Timepiece*, Los Angeles, 1994. *Courtesy of Kenny Rogers*

THE NEW CHRISTY MINSTRELS

Kirby Stone recommended Rogers for the New Christy Minstrels, a high-profile folk group seeking to replace departing members. Rogers was hungry to advance his career. "In a way," he said, "it was a calculated gamble to get my name out there, always in the context of a group, of course." For the versatile singer, changing musical styles wasn't hard: "The folk music I was learning to sing and play . . . wasn't a whole lot different from standard hymns like 'Will the Circle Be Unbroken' and 'I'll Fly Away' that we sang on my grandfather's front porch."

Rogers liked living in Los Angeles, the Minstrels' home base and a music industry hub. But their record label discouraged them from recording original songs and sometimes used professional studio singers, thus limiting royalties. As Rogers put it, "My career was never going to go anywhere with the New Christy Minstrels."

The New Christy Minstrels, c. 1966.
Standing, left to right: Mike Settle, Mark Holly, Kim Carnes, Michael McGuiness, Kyoto Ito, Kenny Rogers.
Seated: Bob Buchanan, Terry Williams, Peter Morse.
Courtesy of Kenny Rogers

Top: 1966 LP cover.

Above: The New Christy Minstrels, c. 1966. Kenny Rogers is seated, third from right.

Right: The New Christy Minstrels, 1966. Kenny Rogers at top.
All images courtesy of Kenny Rogers

Kenny Rogers and the First Edition, c. 1973.
Standing, left to right: Gene Lorenzo, Terry Williams, Jimmy Hassell, Mickey Jones. Seated: Mary Arnold, Kenny Rogers.

Courtesy of Kenny Rogers / Photo by Ed Caraeff

THE FIRST EDITION

Detail of denim shirt with rhinestones and studs,
made by Tony Alamo of Nashville and worn by
Kenny Rogers in the First Edition in the 1970s.
Courtesy of Kenny Rogers / Photo by Bob Delevante

Between 1967 and 1975, Kenny Rogers changed musical directions again with the First Edition—a group that flourished alongside the Byrds and other California bands incorporating elements of rock, folk, and country. Thelma Camacho, Mike Settle, and Terry Williams—all former New Christy Minstrels—started this new act, but at first they didn't want to include the older and less hip-looking Rogers. Rogers changed their minds by sporting a gold earring and a pair of rose-tinted glasses. He also knew that he heard complex harmonies "better than anyone they could find."

Reprise Records producer Jimmy Bowen auditioned the group and liked what he heard. Settle found the words "first edition" in a library book, and Bowen assigned production duties to now-legendary composer Mike Post. Adding energetic drummer Mickey Jones gave the act a more rock-based sound and a livelier stage presence.

Manager Ken Kragen lined up network TV appearances, and from 1971 to 1973 the First Edition anchored *Rollin' on the River*, a syndicated TV series taped in Toronto. This program featured big-name guests such as B. B. King and Kris Kristofferson. Broad exposure helped the band enjoy a #5 pop hit in 1968 with Mickey Newbury's psychedelic "Just Dropped In (To See What Condition My Condition Was In)." A Top Twenty pop hit, Settle's "But You Know I Love You," followed in 1969.

Continued on page 27

Promotional newsletter from the First Edition's label, Reprise Records, c. 1967. *Courtesy of Sharman Pirkle and Susan Bradley*

The First Edition's self-titled debut LP, 1967.

> "I wanted to be accepted in the group . . . and *by* the group—peer approval mattered more to me than public acceptance."

ROCK & POP

KENNY ROGERS & THE FIRST EDITION

KENNY ROGERS AND THE FIRST EDITION
FRIDAY, MAY 22 8:00 P.M.
CAROLINA THEATRE
WINSTON-SALEM
75¢ Souvenir PROGRAM

Top: clockwise, from top: Mary Arnold, Kin Vassy, Kenny Rogers, Terry Williams, Mickey Jones, c. 1970.
Courtesy of Sharman Pirkle and Susan Bradley

Above: Program from Kenny Rogers and the First Edition's concert in Winston-Salem, North Carolina, May 22, 1970.
Courtesy of Sharman Pirkle and Susan Bradley

Left: 1968 magazine ad for Alcoa's Soft Drink Sweepstakes, which offered a concert by the First Edition as part of its $10,000 grand prize.
Courtesy of Sharman Pirkle and Susan Bradley

KENNY ROGERS and THE FIRST EDITION

CHANGING THE FIRST EDITION'S NAME

"It was hard trying to establish a musical identity with four singers singing lead at different times. Kenny had a credible, commercial voice, and I wanted the group's name to be 'Kenny Rogers and the First Edition' so the public would identify with him. I met with Kenny and told him how I felt. He said, 'OK, but you're gonna tell the others.' I said, 'No, *you* are.' So he told 'em, but the fact that the change came from me made it easier for him to break the news.

The concept of a group with three guys and a girl wasn't unusual; Kenny was the key to making the group different. He had one of the most commercial voices in the business—a distinctive voice that made people listen. Just as important, he had the ability to know a good song, and which songs were best for him. He hunted songs all the tiame, and he was hip to Nashville writers as well as writers on the West Coast."

—*Jimmy Bowen*

Above: Promo photo, 1969. *Courtesy of Kenny Rogers*

Bowen changed the group's name to "Kenny Rogers and the First Edition" so the public could identify the act with its lead singer. The band notched a 1969 crossover hit with Mel Tillis's "Ruby, Don't Take Your Love to Town," and their renditions of Mac Davis's "Something's Burning" and Alex Harvey's "Tell It All Brother" reached the pop Top Twenty in 1970. Further hits eluded them, however, and the group dissolved by late 1975.

Denim stage costume worn by Rogers in the First Edition in the 1970s.
Courtesy of Kenny Rogers / Photo by Bob Delevante

Rollin' was released in 1973 on Jolly Rogers Records, the MGM-distributed label run by Kenny Rogers and his brother Lelan from 1972 to 1974.
Courtesy of Sharman Pirkle and Susan Bradley

MATCHMAKER

"As a former member of Kenny Rogers and the First Edition, I know most people have no idea that Kenny is a successful matchmaker as well as a great performer and songwriter. In fact, he introduced me to my husband, Roger Miller.

"Kenny wanted me to meet Roger, but I told Kenny I would *not* go on a blind date. A few days later, Kenny called and said he had arranged for us to go to Margo's birthday party. (Margo was Kenny's wife at the time). I refused, but Kenny said he and Margo would pick me up at six o'clock. I thought, 'When they arrive, I'll just tell them I can't go.' Well, they came over, and Kenny said, 'You're going! Just put something on.' I went, but I was so ornery I refused to get dressed up. I wore a horrible, long, blue patchwork dress. And I made Kenny promise that right after dinner he and Margo would take me home.

"When we finished, Roger asked me, 'Shall we go?' I told him, 'It's Margo's birthday, and I should really go home with Margo and Kenny.' Roger told me he had already asked Kenny if he could take me home, and Kenny had said it would be no problem. I couldn't *believe* it! Kenny was going to *pay* for this one! On the way, Roger took me to see his friend Charles Fleischer perform at the Troubadour. I remember glancing at Roger and thinking there was something so familiar about him.

"When I got home, I called my best friend and told her that I didn't know how or when, but I was going to end up with that man. Roger and I completed each other…Who would have thought that horrible blind date would turn out like it did? We dated for a couple of years, and on February 14, 1978, we married. Our marriage lasted until he passed away, in 1992.

"OK, maybe this one time you were right…Thank you, Kenny."

—*Mary Miller*

Facing page: Roger and Mary Miller on the balcony of L'Ermitage Beverly Hills hotel, early 1980s.

KENNY ROGERS *the* GAMBLER

Kenny Rogers's then-manager, Ken Kragen, was responsible for the cover of *The Gambler* album. Kragen used it to sell CBS-TV executives on the idea of a TV movie starring Rogers. Airing in 1980, *Kenny Rogers As The Gambler* received extremely high ratings and established his iconic image.

LO-934

Detail of jacket and vest worn by Rogers in the 1983 TV movie
Kenny Rogers As The Gambler: The Adventure Continues.
Photo by Bob Delevante

STORYTELLER

Kenny Rogers's distinctive voice and impressive vocal range made him a natural interpreter of country story songs such as the First Edition hits "Ruby, Don't Take Your Love to Town" and "Ruben James."

After Nashville label head Larry Butler signed Rogers to United Artists Records in 1975, top label executives wanted him to stick to country-pop. But Butler and manager Ken Kragen pressed them to release the decidedly country "Lucille," Hal Bynum and Roger Bowling's story of a couple's painful break up. The 1977 crossover hit ignited Rogers's solo career, sending his record sales and concert grosses skyward.

In 1978, lightning struck again with "The Gambler," penned by struggling Nashville songwriter Don Schlitz. Many artists passed up the riveting musical tale, fearing it was too long for radio airplay. Rogers thought otherwise: "The minute I heard the sing-along chorus I knew we had a shot at something big. Audiences love to sing along." A #1 country hit, "The Gambler" also went #16 pop, won a basketful of industry awards, and led to five hugely popular television movies.

Rogers had another chart-topping crossover hit in 1979–80 with Bowling and Billy Edd Wheeler's "Coward of the County," in which a young man takes revenge on three brothers who raped his sweetheart. It, too, inspired a TV movie.

Above left: Mel Tillis's song about a wounded Vietnam War veteran, "Ruby, Don't Take Your Love to Town," was the title track of the first album to bill the group as Kenny Rogers and the First Edition.

Below left: Sheet music for Alex Harvey and Barry Etris's "Ruben James," a Top Forty pop hit in 1969.
Courtesy of Sharman Pirkle and Susan Bradley

> ## "I had the kind of voice and vocal style that could make lyrics both understood and felt."

In 1999 Rogers released another Don Schlitz story song, "The Greatest," on Rogers's own Dreamcatcher Records. In this narrative, a little boy tosses a baseball into the air but repeatedly fails to hit it with his bat. Undiscouraged, he proclaims, "I am the greatest, that is understood, but even I didn't know I could pitch that good!"

Above right: Don Schlitz and Kenny Rogers co-authored this book, based on Rogers's 1999 hit "The Greatest." *Courtesy of Kenny Rogers*

Right: Rawlings baseball, with Rogers's autograph and the logo for his 1999 *The Greatest* tour. *Photo by Bob Delevante*

Below right: Playing cards used to promote the 1988 Kenny Rogers Western Collection clothing line. *Courtesy of Sharman Pirkle and Susan Bradley*

Below left: Rogers's portrayal of the "Gambler" spawned a series of paperback novels based on the popular TV movies. *Courtesy of Sharman Pirkle and Susan Bradley*

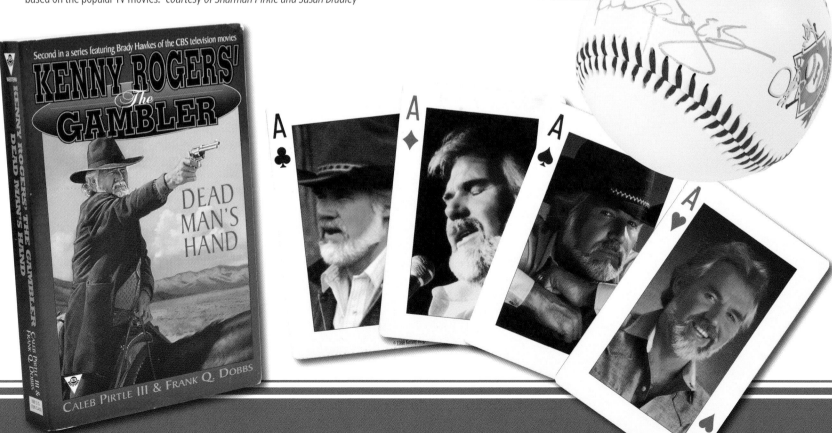

"LUCILLE"

"'Lucille'" began in Norfolk, Virginia, in 1958 when I was serving in the Navy Reserve. I was walking up one of the main streets looking for a bar when I met a blind man walking toward me, playing an old guitar and singing. People were supposed to drop coins into a cup filled with pencils that was wired to the neck of his guitar.

"When I finished active duty, I returned to West Texas and eventually moved to Nashville, where I lived the life of a hard-drinking, rough-living songwriter. All the while I wrote songs and pitched them successfully to country artists such as Johnny Cash, Charley Pride, and George Jones.

"But the blind street singer kept coming back into my mind, and I tried to envision a story for a song about him. Finally, I began, 'In Norfolk, Virginia, across from the depot' and wrote about an old blind man with a pet dog—a man who sang to people coming off trains: 'You picked a fine time to leave me Lucille, with four hungry children and a crop in the field.' Although it was a 'slice of life' story, it had too narrow an appeal.

"Two or three years later I met songwriter Roger Bowling. I told him the history of 'Lucille' and sang it to him. 'I think this thing needs to be put into a barroom,' I said. 'And take the dog and old man out of it—make it so everybody can identify with the story. Put some sex in it. Pull it out of Norfolk and put it in Ohio in a radio breakout area.' Roger lit up: 'You're right! It'll be a monster! Nobody can get that hook outta their mind!'

"So I sang the song while Roger played my guitar. I had worked on the intricate rhyme scheme for years and it all went fast, with Roger breaking in to suggest a different word from time to time. There was no change in the melody. It all rolled out and we finished everything but the last verse, which we did the next day in the United Artists Building. After the country disc jockeys pulled it out of the *Kenny Rogers* album, it exploded. Then it crossed over into the pop field and became a world-wide hit."

—*Hal Bynum*

Facing page: Sheet music for Rogers's 1977 smash hit "Lucille." *Courtesy of Sharman Pirkle and Susan Bradley*

LUCILLE

Words and Music by ROGER BOWLING and HAL BYNUM
As Recorded by KENNY ROGERS

PIANO • VOCAL • GUITAR

ATV MUSIC
Administered by

MCA
music publishing
A Division of **MCA** Inc.

7777 West Bluemound Road Milwaukee, Wisconsin 53213

Exclusively Distributed by
Hal Leonard Publishing Corporation

"THE GAMBLER"

"In 1976, I was working nights as a computer operator at Vanderbilt University, sleeping a couple of hours and then hitting Music Row in Nashville. One August day, I went to see a friend, Bob McDill, and suggested that I was in something of a slump. He showed me a new D-tuning on the guitar that I had never written in. I was inspired by the drone effect of that tuning, and wrote three songs in two hours that same afternoon. One of them was 'The Gambler,' but it wasn't finished, and I spent about six weeks trying to figure out how the song would end. One day, I sat down and wrote the last eight lines, and a mere two years later, it was a hit.

"My father died a couple of years before I wrote the song. After his death, I hit sort of a slump, and being basically a rock-and-roll writer, I was writing on somewhat less than deep subjects. All I can figure is that it was my way of dealing with my relationship with my father. He was the best man I ever knew. He wasn't a gambler. I'm not a gambler. He was my dad. That's what the song is to me, and whatever it is to anyone else is fine."

—Don Schlitz

Facing page: Don Schlitz at the 1979 CMA Awards, accepting his Song of the Year trophy for "The Gambler" while Kenny Rogers, the show's host, looks on.

WRITING "COWARD OF THE COUNTY"

"To me, Kenny Rogers is the master storyteller. His timing is perfect, and his voice just pulls you into the song. I became friends with the late Roger Bowling, and we decided to try co-writing a story song for Kenny. Roger said, 'Got any ideas?' I said, 'Not really.' But I was intrigued by the idea of someone coming from behind and winning.

"I thought of the musical *My Fair Lady*. I was pulling for Eliza Doolittle, the young working-class woman with a heavy Cockney accent played by Audrey Hepburn. She was being molded like a piece of clay by the elite, high-society speech instructor played by Rex Harrison. I wanted her to succeed and come out on top. After expressing this to Roger, I asked if he had any ideas. He said, 'Just a title: The Promise.'

"He picked up my guitar and said, 'Mix us a drink.' I made myself a rum and coke and poured Roger half a glass of straight Jack Daniels. When I came back from the kitchen, he said, 'How 'bout this?' He sang, 'Everyone considered him the coward of the county,' and we were off and running.

"We had a problem creating a scene for Tommy, the song's central character, to sing the chorus again. Roger solved it with the line, 'He reached above the fireplace and took down his daddy's picture. As his tears fell on his daddy's face he heard those words again: Promise me son not to do the things I've done.'

"Roger was a hell of a songwriter."

—*Billy Edd Wheeler*

Facing page: Picture sleeve for "Coward of the County," released in Spain as "El Cobarde."
Courtesy of Sharman Pirkle and Susan Bradley

C 006-082807

UA
UNITED ARTISTS RECORDS

El cobarde

Nº 1 en USA en Inglaterra

Kenny Rogers and Dottie West, c. 1979.
Courtesy of Ron Harman

SINGING PARTNERS

"WHEN THE GAME IS ON THE LINE, KENNY WANTS THE BALL."

"Kenny is very competitive. He's like Michael Jordan. When the game is on the line, Kenny wants the ball, and he knows he's going to score. When he's with someone who's a great singer, he'll take his whole performance up to another level. It's one thing to want it; it's another thing to be able to do it. I've seen it time after time over the years. It's not a common thing among artists, but Kenny has the talent and drive to make it happen."

—*Ken Kragen*

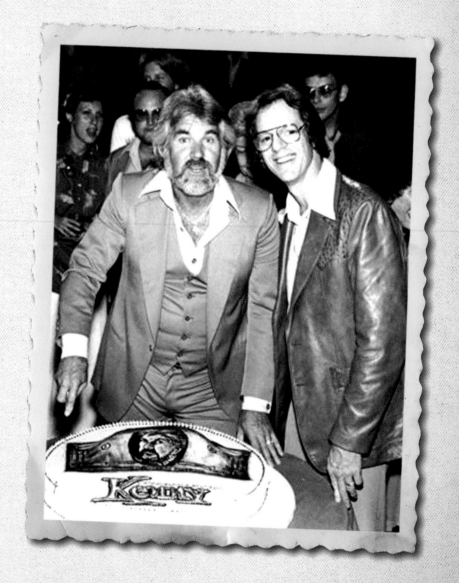

Kenny Rogers and Ken Kragen, c. 1977. *Courtesy of Ken Kragen*

Since the late 1970s, Kenny Rogers has recorded and performed often with artists who reflect his wide-ranging tastes, his sure handling of diverse song material, and his willingness to try various musical approaches. His singing partners have included Dottie West, Kim Carnes, Dolly Parton, Sheena Easton, Lionel Richie, Tim McGraw, and Ronnie Milsap. In addition, he has performed with Anne Murray, Alison Krauss, Billy Dean, Wynonna, Don Henley, and James Ingram.

United Artists Nashville chief Larry Butler introduced West to Rogers at one of her recording sessions, where the two singers spontaneously joined forces on "Every Time Two Fools Collide." In 1978, it became the first of three #1 hits the pair recorded, followed by "All I Ever Need Is You" (1979) and "What Are We Doin' in Love" (1981). "Dottie and I had this great connection," Rogers said. "Part of it might have been that we were both raised in a poor family and yearned for something more."

Continued on page 46

Top right: Kenny Rogers and Dottie West shared a bill at the Silverdome in Pontiac, Michigan, 1978.
Courtesy of Ron Harman

Right: Bob Mackie outfit worn by Dottie West in performance with Kenny Rogers.
Courtesy of Ron Harman / Photo by Bob Delevante

Left: Songbook for Kenny Rogers and Dottie West's album of duets, *Every Time Two Fools Collide* (1978).
Courtesy of Sharman Pirkle and Susan Bradley

Right: Kenny Rogers and Dottie West accepting their 1979 CMA Vocal Duo awards.

SINGING WITH KENNY

"In 1980, Kenny asked Dave Ellingson and me to write a concept album for him. We wrote with Kenny's voice and style of singing in our heads—every melody, the cadence of the words, how they were phrased and sung. He wanted his character to be a modern-day cowboy. We gave him the name Gideon Tanner. Gideon was a bit of a rogue, unable to be faithful to Nell, the only woman he ever loved who loved him in return. The album begins at Gideon's funeral with the church choir singing 'Goin' Home to the Rock.'

"The story then takes the listener through all the stages of Gideon's life. Two songs speak to his love for Nell, telling her, 'Don't Fall in Love with a Dreamer,' and later telling her she needs a better man whose heart is only 'One Place in the Night.' He lands in jail for cattle rustling and sings about his time in prison, proclaiming that 'These Chains' can't keep him from being a free man. In the final song, Gideon is sitting by the campfire reflecting on his life: 'Sayin' goodbye, ridin' away, sayin' goodbye again, wishing you well, miss you until I come back again next year.'

"We made a demo of the ten songs and played it for Kenny. He asked if I would sing "Don't Fall in Love with a Dreamer" with him as a duet. When we recorded it, we sang our vocals live with the band, with Kenny and I facing each other. It became a Top Five record on the country, pop, and adult contemporary charts. Kenny and I performed 'Dreamer' live in concert many times. Most recently, we sang it together in 2012 at the Ford Theater in the Country Music Hall of Fame and Museum, when he was Artist in Residence there.

"Singing with Kenny is always special because we have been friends and worked together since the 1960s—which makes singing together so natural. Without even thinking about it, we always breathe in the same places."

—*Kim Carnes*

Facing page: Kim Carnes and Kenny Rogers at the Country Music Hall of Fame and Museum, May 2012.
Photo by Donn Jones

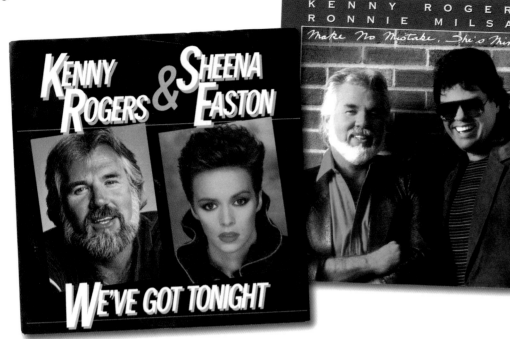

Picture sleeves for Rogers's 1983 chart-topping duet with Sheena Easton, "We've Got Tonight," and Rogers and Ronnie Milsap's "Make No Mistake, She's Mine," a #1 hit in 1987.

Courtesy of Sharman Pirkle and Susan Bradley

Rogers's bond with Dolly Parton was strengthened by their duet "Islands in the Stream," which topped the country and pop charts in 1983. In the early 1980s, the duo drew huge audiences in the U.S. and overseas. Rogers's 2013 Warner Bros. album, *You Can't Make Old Friends*, featured Parton on the title track.

During the 1980s, Rogers recorded duet hits with Carnes ("Don't Fall in Love with a Dreamer"), Easton ("We've Got Tonight"), and Milsap ("Make No Mistake, She's Mine"). "Buy Me a Rose," featuring Rogers, Krauss, and Dean, became a #1 hit during 1999–2000.

Far left: Sheet music for "Lady."
Courtesy of Sharman Pirkle and Susan Bradley

Left: Rogers with Lionel Richie, who wrote and produced "Lady," Rogers's 1980 single that topped *Billboard*'s country, pop, and adult contemporary charts.
Courtesy of Sharman Pirkle and Susan Bradley

"I've always felt that I sing so much better in duets than I do by myself"

Left: Velvet jacket and gown with rhinestones and beads, worn by Dolly Parton when she performed "Islands in the Stream" with Rogers on her TV series *Dolly*, in 1988.
Courtesy of Dolly Parton / Photo by Bob Delevante

Above: Rogers wore this Bill Whitten bugle-beaded jacket when he sang with Dolly Parton in the 1985 TV special "Kenny Rogers and Dolly Parton: Together."
Courtesy of Kenny Rogers / Photo by Bob Delevante

Top: Picture sleeve for "Islands in the Stream."
Courtesy of Sharman Pirkle and Susan Bradley

Bottom: Dolly Parton and Kenny Rogers, c. 1990.
Courtesy of Kenny Rogers

RECORDING "LUCILLE"

"We went into the studio every night for a week and cut the album *Kenny Rogers*. Every night, I tried to get Kenny to do a song called 'Lucille' . . . He said, 'Larry, I know it's a country hit, but I think it's too country for me.' On the last night . . . we had about fifteen minutes left. We had enough songs for the album, and Kenny said, 'Okay, I guess that's it.' I said, 'No, we've got time to do "Lucille."'

"We rehearsed it one time. Kenny said, 'I've got to tell you something that I really don't like about it . . . The guy leaves the bar with her and goes up to her hotel room. How could he do that right after her husband was standing there and saying "You picked a fine time to leave me."'. . . I said, 'Well, what would you say?'

"Kenny's reply changed the entire ending of the song; and the word change was exactly what the song needed to say. 'She was a beauty, but when she came to me, she must have thought I'd lost my mind. I couldn't hold her, for the words that he told her, kept comin' back time after time.' Kenny rewrote that part of the song right on the spot, and that is the version we recorded that night . . . It was an inspirational change that made total sense of the story. So in the very first take, during the waning minutes of the last recording session for the album, the song 'Lucille' finally made its way onto the album.

"Most people wouldn't know that Kenny re-wrote that last verse, but he's a great songwriter. In fact, he has written many hits throughout the years—not only for himself, but for others as well."

—*Larry Butler*

Facing page: Kenny Rogers and Larry Butler, United Artists Records, c. 1979.
Courtesy of Peggy Butler

Kenny Rogers, c. 1975

Detail of leather vest with half-dollar buttons, a gift to Rogers from a fan.

Courtesy of Kenny Rogers / Photo by Bob Delevante

RECORDING ARTIST

PRODUCING AN OLD FRIEND

"In the early 1970s, I joined Shiloh, a Texas group that had moved to California and was looking for a new keyboardist. Kenny was producing this band for Amos Records, Jimmy Bowen's label, and Jimmy was producing Kenny Rogers and the First Edition for the Warner Bros. affiliate Reprise Records. Kenny moved on to other labels, but after I began running Warner's Nashville office in 1984—and Kenny left RCA—I re-signed him to Reprise. He laughed and said, 'Hey! When you were with Shiloh, I was producing you!' Both of us enjoyed working together again. Kenny not only had a unique vocal style, he was also a great song man—a real plus for a recording artist. He understood songs and how they were constructed, because he was a songwriter himself. And as an artist, he knew what he was singing about. We didn't score a major hit, but we got him back on the charts from 1989 into 1992, and cracked the country Top Ten with 'The Vows Go Unbroken' in 1989.

"We had a good time, too. He always came in ready to go, even if he wasn't feeling well. But work never got in the way of self-expression. Kenny knew the process of making a record, and wasn't put off by difficult moments. He was prepared to put himself 100 percent in the hands of his partners. He considered me his partner, and trusted that I would have his best interests in mind. He knew how to rely on the flow of the present moment. He would always listen with an open heart and mind to others' ideas. If his performance was off, he'd be the first to say, 'Let's do this again; we can do it better.' We could accomplish a great deal without a lot being said, because Kenny is smart. And he's relentless in his pursuit of excellence."

—*Jim Ed Norman*

Facing page:
Top: Jim Ed Norman and Kenny Rogers, c. 1990.
Bottom: Shiloh single produced by Rogers, 1970.
Courtesy of Jim Ed Norman

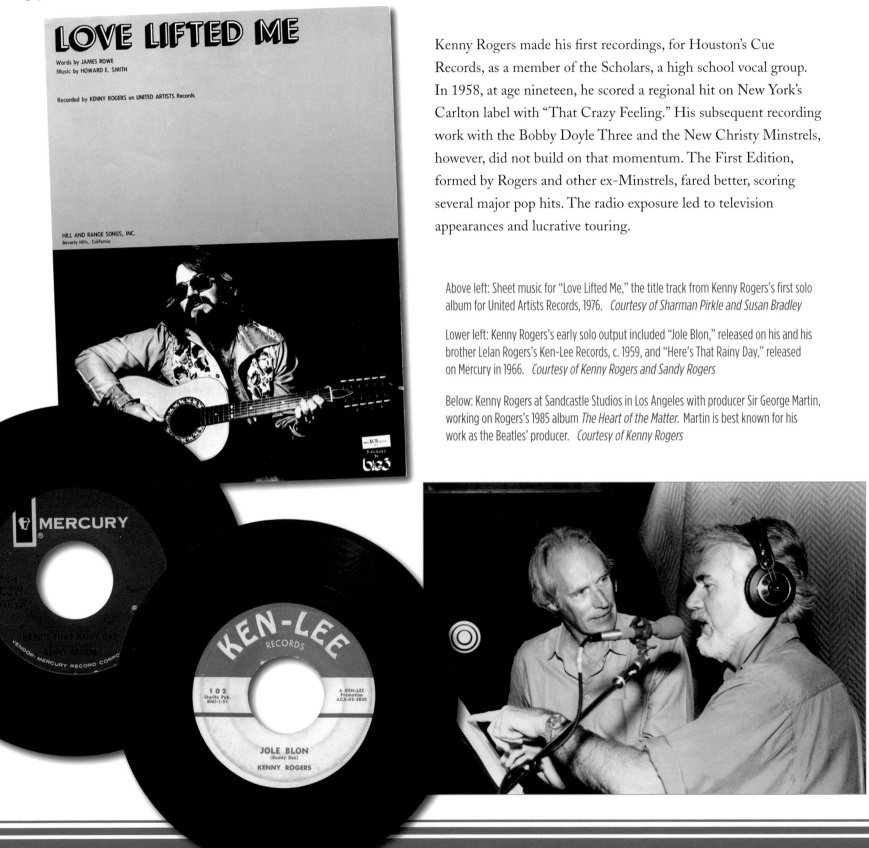

Kenny Rogers made his first recordings, for Houston's Cue Records, as a member of the Scholars, a high school vocal group. In 1958, at age nineteen, he scored a regional hit on New York's Carlton label with "That Crazy Feeling." His subsequent recording work with the Bobby Doyle Three and the New Christy Minstrels, however, did not build on that momentum. The First Edition, formed by Rogers and other ex-Minstrels, fared better, scoring several major pop hits. The radio exposure led to television appearances and lucrative touring.

Above left: Sheet music for "Love Lifted Me," the title track from Kenny Rogers's first solo album for United Artists Records, 1976. *Courtesy of Sharman Pirkle and Susan Bradley*

Lower left: Kenny Rogers's early solo output included "Jole Blon," released on his and his brother Lelan Rogers's Ken-Lee Records, c. 1959, and "Here's That Rainy Day," released on Mercury in 1966. *Courtesy of Kenny Rogers and Sandy Rogers*

Below: Kenny Rogers at Sandcastle Studios in Los Angeles with producer Sir George Martin, working on Rogers's 1985 album *The Heart of the Matter*. Martin is best known for his work as the Beatles' producer. *Courtesy of Kenny Rogers*

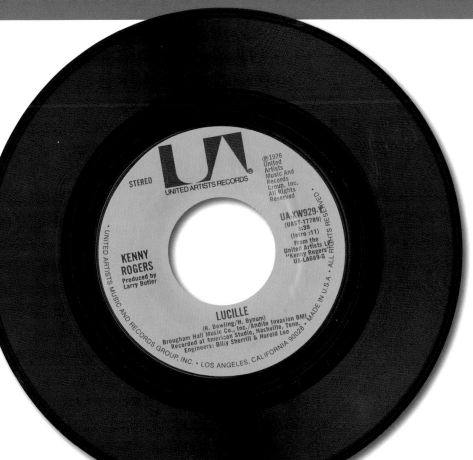

Rogers emerged as a star in his own right in 1977 with his first #1 record, the international crossover smash "Lucille." The first of twenty-one *Billboard* country chart-topping discs—many of them crossover hits— "Lucille" launched a solo career that has generated sales of more than 51 million albums in the United States alone. Follow-up hits, including his own recordings and duets with the likes of Dottie West, Sheena Easton, Kim Carnes, and Ronnie Milsap, helped Rogers fill arenas across the nation and overseas.

Left: Rogers's breakout single, "Lucille."

Below left: *Kenny Rogers' Greatest Hits*, released on Liberty Records in 1980.

Below: Kenny Rogers and Ronnie Milsap, 1987. Their recording of "Make No Mistake, She's Mine" won a 1987 Grammy for Best Country Vocal Performance, Duet.

Kenny Rogers, 1983.

Detail of jacket, with bugle-beaded vest by Bon Choix Couture and Bill Whitten shirt, worn by Rogers onstage, c. 1984.

Courtesy of Kenny Rogers / Photo by Bob Delevante

ENTERTAINER

Kenny Rogers had begun performing in public by age ten, when he won a half-gallon of vanilla ice cream in a Houston talent show. "That contest," he recalled, "was one of the first times I felt the thrill of performing." Rogers graduated to professional status with a high school vocal group, the Scholars, who played local shows and recorded briefly for Houston's Cue label.

Rogers further honed his entertaining skills with Houston-based jazz combo the Bobby Doyle Three, with Los Angeles–based folk group the New Christy Minstrels, and with country-pop band Kenny Rogers and the First Edition, also based in L.A. As a solo artist, his showmanship and audience rapport made Rogers one of the most successful entertainers in history.

Above right: The Scholars at the University of Houston's Frontier Fiesta, c. 1957. Rogers is second from left. *Courtesy of Kenny Rogers*

Right: Kenny Rogers and Dottie West, c. 1979. *Courtesy of Ron Harman*

Below: One of the tambourines Rogers would throw into the crowd at his concerts. *Courtesy of Kenny Rogers / Photo by Bob Delevante*

ICP/MAGICWORKS ENTERTAINMENT INTERNATIONAL INC

Kenny & Reba
IN CONCERT

FRIDAY APRIL 17TH
PERTH ENTERTAINMENT CENTRE
TICKETS FROM RED TICKETS PHONECHARGE (08) 9484 1222 OR COUNTRY 1800 199 991
CHECK OUT THEIR NEW ALBUMS ON CD & CASSETTE
KENNY ROGERS 'ACROSS MY HEART' OUT NOW ON RHYTHM SAFARI/UNIVERSAL
REBA McENTIRE 'MOMENTS & MEMORIES - THE BEST OF REBA' OUT NOW ON UNIVERSAL

AIR NEW ZEALAND   CMT

KWJJ Announces

Kenny Rogers

PLUS SPECIAL GUEST
Eddie Rabbitt

at the Portland Civic Auditorium
Monday, July 17, 7 & 10 PM

Tickets $8.50, 7.50, 6.50 at the Civic Auditorium Box Office,
Meier & Frank, Stevens at Lloyd Center, Lipmans downtown

From Sounds of the World and the Edgewood Agency

Left: Stage outfit worn by Rogers.
Courtesy of Kenny Rogers
Photo by Bob Delevante

Top Left: Kenny Rogers and Reba McEntire
shared the bill in Perth, Australia, 1998.
Courtesy of Sharman Pirkle
and Susan Bradley

Top right: Poster from a 1989 concert
in Portland, Oregon.
Courtesy of Sharman Pirkle
and Susan Bradley

Right: Rogers at a Farm Aid concert
in Champaign, Illinois, 1985.
Courtesy of Kenny Rogers
Photo by Kelly Junkermann

"KENNY IS A GREAT SHOWMAN"

"Kenny has the ability to take something that happens spontaneously in one show and do it from then on, but always making it real, like it was the first time it happened. During one of his Christmas tours, stagehands were supposed to sprinkle artificial snow flakes when he sang a certain song. When the 'snow' didn't come down, Kenny said, 'Listen, guys, when I say snow, I want it to snow!' Once again the stagehands tried to sprinkle it, but something went wrong. The entire contents of the box of snow fell down at the same time, right on top of Kenny! Kenny repeated that from then on, and audiences loved it.

"At least 50 percent of Kenny's stage appeal is his personality and his ability to talk with the audience—and the audience having this love affair with him. There was one show Kenny did when he had just lost his voice temporarily. There were about 5,000 or 6,000 people in the audience. He went out and told them, 'I haven't got any voice. So my band's gonna play, and you do the singing. If any of you want your money back, that's OK.' I think two people asked for their money back, and everyone else stayed and sang. The audience wants to feel that the show was special, something performed just for them. When something like this happens, the next day people start telling all their friends about it."

—*Ken Kragen*

Facing page: Kenny Rogers, c. 1983.
Photo by Kelly Junkermann

KENNY ROGERS, ENTERTAINER

"If there was a university for country music entertainers, when it comes to Entertaining 101 Kenny Rogers would be the professor of that class. Kenny was sweet enough to give me my first major tour. It ran through the Northeast, where a guy like me might never be given a second chance—or a first one. But when you show up with Kenny Rogers, the red carpet's rolled out. . .

"And night after night, *class was on*. Night after night, you watched the master. As we moved through theaters, we moved to arenas. This is where I saw it . . . This guy is very humble, but Kenny is brilliant . . . The man learned to put the stage in the middle of an arena, because he wanted to *play* to the entire arena.

"But I was smart enough myself to watch every night—watch a man entertain. Watch a man take [hold of] people who had paid their hard-earned money to get away from what's outside that building. And that's what this man taught me. If you want to learn how to entertain, Kenny Rogers will show you."

—*Garth Brooks*

Facing page: Kenny Rogers and Garth Brooks at the Country Music Hall of Fame and Museum's 2013 Medallion Ceremony, where Brooks inducted Rogers into the Hall of Fame. *Photo by Donn Jones*

Reba McEntire and Kenny Rogers on the set of *The Gambler Returns: The Luck of the Draw*, 1991.
Courtesy of Kenny Rogers / Photo by Kelly Junkermann

TELEVISION STAR

SINGING WITH RAY CHARLES

"One of my most memorable duets was never even released on a record. Steve Glassmeyer and I had written a song called 'Lady Luck,' and I performed it on one of my television specials with my idol, Ray Charles. Ray played the piano and we sang it together. I knew once we started, it was an unfair race. He was going to run away from me, but I was going to do everything I could do to keep up . . . Some people sing songs they way they learn them. The greats sing the way they feel. I remember asking him one time, 'How do you know when to do those soulful licks?' As only Ray Charles could put it, 'If you have to think about them, they're wrong.'"

—*Kenny Rogers*

Left to right: Ray Charles, Kenny Rogers, Dottie West, and the Oak Ridge Boys—Joe Bonsall, Duane Allen, William Lee Golden, and Richard Sterban—in the 1979 TV show "A Special Kenny Rogers."

Over the decades, television broadened Kenny Rogers's popularity. After Ken Kragen caught the First Edition's high-energy show at an L.A. club and alerted the Smothers Brothers, whom he was managing, they scheduled the group for their highly rated CBS-TV series, *The Smothers Brothers Comedy Hour*. "TV was especially powerful back then," Kragen said in 2014. "There were only three networks, and the exposure you got from any appearance was much stronger than it is today." Kragen signed the First Edition as a client and booked the band for programs including *The Ed Sullivan Show*, *Rowan & Martin's Laugh-In*, and *The Johnny Cash Show*.

"*The Tonight Show* really broke Kenny's solo career in the mid-1970s," Kragen said. "John Davidson was guest-hosting for Johnny Carson. Kenny is a warm person and a good raconteur, but when John had Kenny take off his rose-colored glasses, it made him even more accessible." Likewise, performing "Lucille" on nationally syndicated *Hee Haw* helped establish Rogers's credibility with country fans. Dozens of specials and his made-for-TV movies further increased his success as a recording artist and touring performer.

Continued on page 68

Top: Rogers on *The Tonight Show Starring Johnny Carson*, c. 1979.
Courtesy of Sandy Rogers

Middle: Rogers on NBC-TV's *Barbara Mandrell and the Mandrell Sisters*, November 1980. Left to right: Irlene Mandrell, Louise Mandrell, Kenny Rogers, Barbara Mandrell.
Courtesy of Sharman Pirkle and Susan Bradley

Bottom: Rogers on *Rollin' on the River*, a syndicated TV series taped in Toronto and anchored by Kenny Rogers and the First Edition from 1971 to 1973.
Courtesy of Kenny Rogers

TV SCENE By GEORGE MAKSIAN

'Gambler' was best bet

IF ANYONE HAD any doubts, Kenny Rogers is still sizzling. His latest TV movie special, "The Gambler—The Adventure Continues," shown in two parts last week on CBS, hit the ratings jackpot. The shows helped power CBS to a smashing victory in the national Nielsen sweepstakes, announced yesterday.

CBS scored its most lopsided victory since the season began 10 weeks ago, with an average prime time 21.0 rating to ABC's 16.5 and NBC's 14.5. A rating point is 1% of the nation's 84 million homes. In the season-to-date averages, CBS has doubled its lead over second-place ABC and is far ahead of NBC. CBS has won seven out of the 10 weeks; ABC has won three.

IN THE WEEK ended Sunday, CBS won six of the seven nights, losing only Wednesday to ABC. All of the competing shows against "The Gambler" finished out of the money. On Monday night, NBC had the movie, "Girls of the White Orchid," which landed in 23d place, out of 66 shows. ABC's Monday Night Football was No. 32.

Tuesday's NBC competition included a rerun of "The A-Team" (No. 58) and "Remington Steele" (No. 35). ABC's "Three's Company" finished in 45th place, while "Oh Madeline" was No. 51. Even the usually strong "Hart to Hart" proved no match for "The Gambler." It wound up in 56th place.

Rogers' first TV movie, "The Gambler," aired on CBS in April 1980 and was the highest-rated TV movie of the season. His second special, "Coward of the County," in October 1981, also topped the ratings charts. The only show seen by more people than his new special so far this season was ABC's "The Day After."

IN THE EVENING NEWS race, CBS' Dan Rather continued his strong

Daily News, Wednesday, December 7, 1983

THE TOP TEN

Here are the ten most popular TV shows, as measured by last week's national Nielsen ratings. The first figure is the percentage of the nation's TV homes. The second is the share of the audience watching TV at the time.

1	"Gambler" II	CBS	29.6	45
2	"Gambler" I	CBS	29.4	42
3	Dallas	CBS	26.6	42
4	60 Minutes	CBS	26.3	39
5	Carson Special	NBC	25.1	34
6	A Team	NBC	24.5	35
7	Dynasty	ABC	24.4	36
8	Simon & Simon	CBS	24.0	36
9	Falcon Crest	CBS	23.0	38
10	Hotel	ABC	22.3	37

lead, with ABC's Peter Jennings a solid second and NBC's Tom Brokaw last. CBS had a 14.3 average, while ABC had a 12.2 and NBC an 11.7. The figures reflect a growing audience interest in network news so far this fall. The combined total for the three networks was unusually high. It was also ABC's best showing since March.

NBC and AB[...] for second plac[...] works started u[...] September. Last [...] ated his newscas[...] also planning a [...]

The fall ratin[...] problem for cab[...] work viewing in [...] million homes [...] thanks to strong [...] and specials. I[...] most successful [...] been suffering [...]

Clipping from New York's *Daily News*, 1983.
Courtesy of Ken Kragen

On the set of the 1985 CBS-TV movie *Wild Horses*.
Left to right: Actors Ben Johnson, David Andrews, Richard Farnsworth, Pam Dawber, Kenny Rogers, and director Dick Lowry.
Courtesy of Kenny Rogers

Television continued to build Rogers's career in the 1990s and beyond. An engaging video was essential in making his rendition of Don Schlitz's "The Greatest" a Top Thirty country hit in 1999. That same year, Rogers's Dreamcatcher label also released "Buy Me a Rose," which he recorded with Alison Krauss and Billy Dean. The song reached #1 after inspiring a February 2000 episode of CBS-TV's *Touched by an Angel* in which Rogers appeared. In the new century, Rogers performed with Dolly Parton, Lionel Richie, Darius Rucker, and other stars in *Kenny Rogers: The First 50 Years*, which aired on GAC in 2011.

"Television proved to be a major force in my career, not only with the First Edition, but also as a solo performer."

Left: The Association for Independent Music 2000 Indie Award for Short Form Video, presented to Rogers and his record label, for "The Greatest." *Courtesy of Kenny Rogers / Photo by Bob Delevante*

Top: Ken Kragen and Kenny Rogers at a TV rehearsal. *Courtesy of Ken Kragen*

Bottom: Rogers taped a segment of his 1980 TV special *Kenny Rogers America* with Super Bowl champions the Pittsburgh Steelers. Clockwise from right: Terry Bradshaw, "Mean" Joe Greene, Rogers, Rocky Bleier, Lynn Swann. *Courtesy of Kenny Rogers*

Rogers as Brady Hawkes in
Kenny Rogers As The Gambler.

Courtesy of Kenny Rogers

ACTOR

Reba McEntire and Kenny Rogers in *The Gambler Returns: The Luck of the Draw* (1991).

"I'M A HUGE KENNY ROGERS FAN"

"I played a headlining role in one of Kenny's *Gambler* movies, *The Gambler Returns*, in 1991. The best parts of doing the movie were the times we got to sit for a while, waiting on our scene to begin, and visit. He always had the best stories and jokes to tell all of us. And I do mean all of us. It didn't matter if a grip or one of the main stars of the film were there, he treated everyone the same. I love that about Kenny.

"If you don't know by now, I'm a huge Kenny Rogers fan! I love his music, his singing, his great outlook on life, his photography talent, his wit . . . he's a total sweetheart!"

—*Reba*

"I think that my talent in this area is that I'm good at being me in different clothes."

Although Kenny Rogers appeared in the TV movie *The Dream Makers* (1975)—for which the First Edition provided the soundtrack—his acting career took off when his 1978 crossover hit "The Gambler" inspired the first of five made-for-television movies broadcast between 1980 and 1994. Each production developed Rogers's character, Brady Hawkes, and reinforced the singer's iconic Gambler image. References to real-life events and authentic heroes were "part of the believability that allowed me to pull off the role," Rogers said.

"Coward of the County" inspired its own televised movie, first aired in 1981. Rogers plays small-town preacher Matthew Spencer, whose nephew Tommy is torn between honoring his father's advice to shun violence and punishing the men who raped his sweetheart.

Continued on page 74

Top left: Rogers in
Coward of the County, 1981.

Left: Bandoleer with holster,
worn by Rogers in *The Gambler*
TV movies.
Courtesy of Kenny Rogers
Photo by Bob Delevante

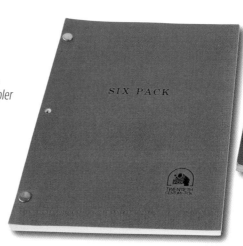

Left: Bruce Boxleitner, Linda Gray, and Kenny Rogers in
Kenny Rogers As The Gambler, Part III: The Legend Continues (1987).

Right: Rogers's scripts to the film *Six Pack* and the 1983 TV movie
Kenny Rogers As The Gambler: The Adventure Continues.
Courtesy of Sharman Pirkle and Susan Bradley / Photo by Bob Delevante

Rogers further polished his acting skills as race car driver Brewster Baker in the theatrical release *Six Pack* (1982). On television, he played former rodeo champion Matt Cooper in *Wild Horses* (1985) and photographer Frank Morgan in *Christmas in America* (1990). His TV acting credits also include bounty hunter Quentin Leech in *Rio Diablo* (1993) and gambling con man Jack MacShayne in two 1994 *MacShayne* productions.

Rogers made his stage debut in Athens, Georgia, in 1998, starring as store owner Hank Longley in *The Toy Shoppe*. Later presented at New York's venerable Beacon Theater, the one-act play was written by Rogers and his versatile assistant, Kelly Junkermann. Based on Rogers's childhood experiences at Bryant's Five-and-Dime in Houston, where Mr. Bryant told stories about the value of old toys, the play stresses "love, faith, and appreciation for the value of every individual," Rogers said. The singer has long made it a part of his holiday tours, and in 2013 country singer Billy Dean filled the starring role in a production staged in Branson, Missouri.

Top: Lobby card for the 1982 film *Six Pack*.
Courtesy of Sharman Pirkle and Susan Bradley

Middle: Die-cast metal replica of the Camaro driven by Rogers in *Six Pack*.
Courtesy of Sharman Pirkle and Susan Bradley / Photo by Bob Delevante

Right: Erin Gray and Kenny Rogers in *Six Pack*.

"THERE ARE BROADLY TWO KINDS OF ACTORS."

"My theory of acting, for what it's worth, is that there are broadly two kinds of actors. First there are people who can act. You give them some unbelievable dialogue in an unbelievable situation, and they can make it totally believable. And they can embody a thousand different characters. And then there are actors like me. Give me believable dialogue in a believable situation and I can keep it believable."

—*Kenny Rogers*

Scene from *Kenny Rogers As The Gambler* (1980). *Courtesy of Kenny Rogers*

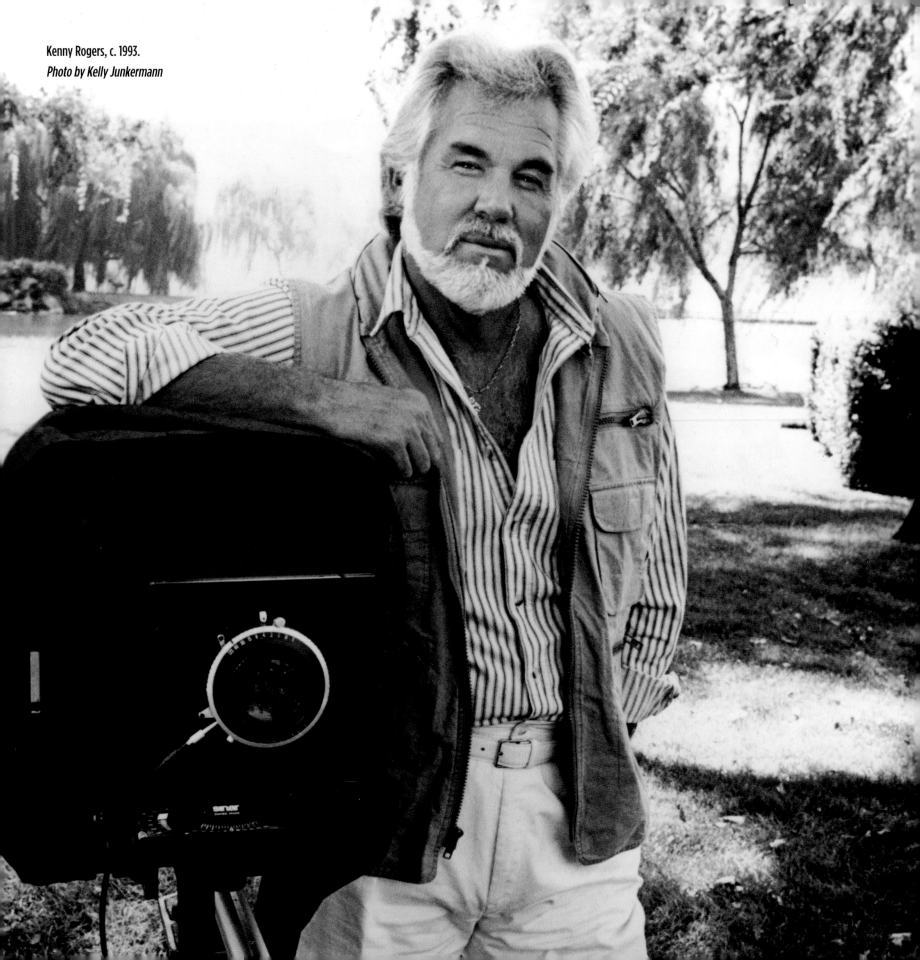

Kenny Rogers, c. 1993.
Photo by Kelly Junkermann

Detail of Swingster windbreaker with Rogers logo, sold through Rogers's fan club, early 1980s.
Courtesy of Kenny Rogers / Photo by Bob Delevante

PHOTOGRAPHER

Top left: Kenny Rogers and Rob Pincus,
British Columbia, late 1980s.
Courtesy of Kelly Junkermann

Top right: Rogers in Pennsylvania, early 1990s.
Courtesy of Kelly Junkermann

Left: Rogers at Yosemite National Park,
late 1990s.
Courtesy of Kenny Rogers

All photos by Kelly Junkermann

Kenny Rogers's fascination with photography began in the 1960s while working with the Bobby Doyle Three and Kirby Stone's band: "Kirby introduced me to Milton Greene, the famous high-fashion photographer whose subjects included Marilyn Monroe, Frank Sinatra, and Judy Garland." Years later, Rogers spent a week in the darkroom learning from John Sexton, assistant to famed landscape photographer Ansel Adams, and he learned portrait photography from the world-renowned Yousuf Karsh.

Honorary Master of Photography award presented to Rogers by the Professional Photographers of America (PPA), 2014.
Courtesy of Kenny Rogers / Photo by Bob Delevante

Honorary Master
of Photography
Hon. M. Photog
Presented to
Kenny Rogers
January, 2014

"Photography opened a whole new door for me, and I embraced it."

According to Rogers's former manager Ken Kragen, "Kenny approaches anything he gets excited about by devoting enormous amounts of time to it. He's determined to be good at it." As Rogers explained, "Artists need outside interests to help balance the unreal lives they are living . . . Photography has been an extension of my creative self, but it has also offered me an escape from the scrutiny of the public eye and the craziness of a concert tour."

In 1986 Rogers published the best of his travel photos in *Kenny Rogers' America*, a collection of images in the Ansel Adams tradition. In 1987 he followed with *Your Friends and Mine*, selected from his many portrait photos of celebrities including Ray Charles, Elizabeth Taylor, and Bob Hope. Rogers later showcased portrait photos of country music stars in *This Is My Country* (2005).

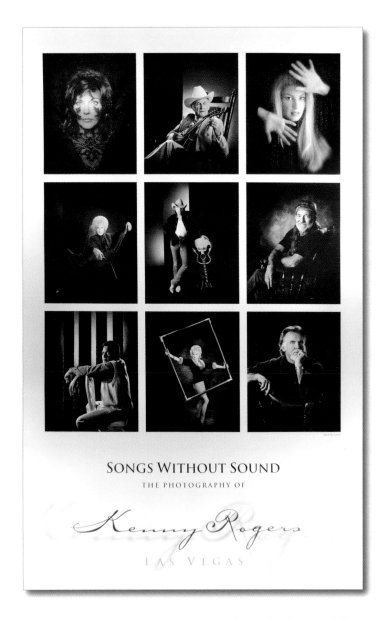

SONGS WITHOUT SOUND

THE PHOTOGRAPHY OF

Kenny Rogers

LAS VEGAS

Above left: Rogers examining a poster for *Kenny Rogers' America*, an exhibition of his photography at the Country Music Hall of Fame and Museum in 1987.

Above: Poster for an exhibition of Rogers's photographs of country music artists, Las Vegas, 2001. *Courtesy of Kenny Rogers*

"WE WERE KENNY'S SHERPAS"

"When Kenny became passionate about photography, he spent three days in the darkroom with John Sexton, who had assisted world-famous landscape photographer Ansel Adams. Kenny was hooked! This was no ordinary point-and-shoot method. He now used a larger camera and film and a complicated "zone" system of shooting and developing the film.

"Like playing tennis, shooting photos with Kenny followed a brutal schedule. He was living in Athens, Georgia, at the time, flying in and out for every concert. We would fly into a town, rent a vehicle, and start our quest for an interesting photograph. Most of the local people thought their town didn't have anything special, but Kenny would find the beauty in an old bridge, abandoned railroad tracks, a cemetery, or a lonely tree.

"Rob Pincus was Kenny's driver and security guard. Usually, Rob would get lost, and that's how we'd find the picture. We were Kenny's Sherpas, lugging around the heavy camera gear. Kenny would take the shot, do his concert, and fly home.

"We'd get in around midnight and go straight to the darkroom and develop the film. Kenny couldn't wait until morning for it to dry, so he'd use a hair dryer to get it done faster. Adams's system isn't easy, and we would spend hours getting the perfect print.

"The next morning Kenny would mount and frame the photograph. By the next day's concert, we were not only off to look for the next great treasure a town had to offer—he would also be showing the band a finished framed print from the day before! Kenny had discovered the beauty that most people in the town did not know existed in their own backyard."

—*Kelly Junkermann*

Facing page: Rogers in an Illinois coal mine, late 1980s.
Courtesy of Kelly Junkermann / Photo by Kelly Junkermann

Top left: Barber shop, Clarksville, Tennessee.   Top right: Minnie Pearl, from *This Is My Country*, 2005.

Bottom right: "Harry and Bob on the Bowery, New York, New York," from *Kenny Rogers' America*, 1986.
Courtesy of Kenny Rogers / Photos by Kenny Rogers

Below: Rogers used this Linhof Master Technika Classic camera, with its unconventional
4x5" format, to capture the studio portraits of country music artists for *This Is My Country*.
Courtesy of Kenny Rogers / Photo by Bob Delevante

Far left:
Portrait photographer
Yousuf Karsh, from
Your Friends and Mine, 1987.

Left:
Miles Davis.

Below:
"Ramshackle House,
Athens, Georgia," from
Kenny Rogers' America.

Courtesy of Kenny Rogers
Photos by Kenny Rogers

Rogers with children and parents at the
Kenny Rogers Children's Center, March 2012.
*Courtesy of Kenny Rogers Children's Center,
Sikeston, Missouri*

HUMANITARIAN

"WE PLAYED TONS OF CHARITY EVENTS"

"In the late 1970s, when I was the head tennis pro at Amelia Island, Florida, a singer came to the resort and wanted to take some lessons. It was Kenny Rogers, and he was *awful*. But I quickly learned something: He would do whatever it took to get better. I taught him for the week, and when he left he gave me his number: 'If you ever come to Los Angeles, give me a call.'

"So when I was visiting friends in L.A., I did. 'Come on over,' he said. 'Let's play some tennis.' We went to visit one of his buddies and played; four hours later it was dark and we stopped. Kenny had gotten better.

"He asked me what I was doing now, and I said, 'I was playing the pro tour, but I've run out of money so I'm going back to teaching.' Kenny said, 'I've got an idea. I'll sponsor you, and when you're not on the pro tour you'll go on tour with me and teach me and the band.'

"A typical day in L.A. was four hours of tennis in the morning, quesadillas for lunch, and four more hours of tennis in the afternoon. His stamina was unbelievable! We played everybody—Johnny Carson, Bill Cosby, Robert Duvall—and Kenny quickly became one of the top celebrity players. Eventually, he earned a world ranking in doubles on the Association of Tennis Professionals tour.

"We played tons of charity events. In Cincinnati, Ohio, before a sold-out concert, we played an event where teams donated a thousand dollars each to play us. We played sixteen sets of tennis, winning fifteen of them. I was ready to collapse and die; Kenny went on and did his two-hour concert a few hours later."

—*Kelly Junkermann*

Facing page: Kenny Rogers, c. 1980. *Photo by Kelly Junkermann*

As Kenny Rogers's career progressed, his love of sports fueled his interest in humanitarian projects. With tennis instructor Kelly Junkermann, he competed in hundreds of charity matches while on tour. At his estate near Athens, Georgia, Rogers created the Gambler's Invitational, a multi-sport fundraiser including golf, tennis, basketball, and fishing. Celebrities and professional athletes paid $500 to play, and public ticket sales raised additional sums. Renamed Kenny Rogers Classic Weekend, it became a family event that sponsors sustained for a number of years. Proceeds funded the Athens Area Homeless Shelter.

"Kenny grew up in the projects in Houston," former manager Ken Kragen said. "He knows what poverty is like. Working to reduce hunger and homelessness came naturally to him." Building on singer Harry Chapin's efforts, in 1982 Rogers and then-wife Marianne pledged $1 million to establish the World Hunger Media Awards, which recognize print and broadcast media coverage of this problem. The awards were later renamed in Chapin's honor.

With Rogers's financial and artistic support, Kragen was instrumental in organizing the multi-artist 1985 charity recording "We Are the World," which raised millions for hunger relief in Africa. Rogers was also front-and-center in the Kragen brainchild "Hands Across America," a campaign to raise funds for—and public awareness of—hunger and homelessness in the U.S.

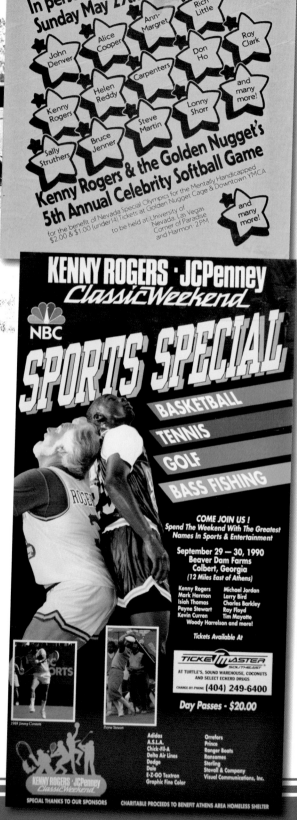

Above: Kenny Rogers and Tanya Tucker at one of Rogers's celebrity softball charity games, late 1970s.

Above right: Kenny Rogers's annual celebrity softball game, a fundraiser for the Nevada Special Olympics, was held in Las Vegas in 1990.
Courtesy of Ken Kragen

Right: Rogers with basketball star Michael Jordan in a 1990 poster for Kenny Rogers Classic Weekend. This event was televised by NBC.
Courtesy of Sharman Pirkle and Susan Bradley

"Success without sharing is unacceptable."

Because of Rogers's longtime support for the United Cerebral Palsy Center in Sikeston, Missouri, in 2000 the facilty changed its name to the Kenny Rogers Children's Center. It treats children at no charge to the families served.

Above: Kenny Rogers and Keller Breuer at the Kenny Rogers Children's Center, March 2012.   *Courtesy of Kenny Rogers Children's Center*

Top right: Lead sheet for "We Are the World," signed by Kenny Rogers, Diana Ross, Harry Chapin, Daryl Hall, Tina Turner, Quincy Jones, and other participants in the recording, 1985.   *Courtesy of Ken Kragen*

Bottom right: Recording session for "We Are the World," 1985. Left to right: Lionel Richie, Stevie Wonder, Paul Simon, James Ingram (partly hidden), Kenny Rogers, Tina Turner, and Billy Joel.

KENNY ROGERS CLASSIC WEEKEND

"Kenny held a tennis charity event on his estate near Athens, Georgia, but soon we wanted to expand it. Kenny was now into golf and had built a golf course. Yes, he built a golf course—a full eighteen holes! We had also played a lot of basketball on the road. In fact, Garth Brooks's first tour was with Kenny and every day we would find the local YMCA and Kenny and his crew would battle Garth and his crew in a pickup basketball game.

"One day I asked Kenny, 'Remember when you were a kid and all your buddies came over and everybody was good at something different? Well, imagine that they all grew up and now they were all the best in the world. You became a singer, Jimmy Connors played tennis, Michael Jordan played basketball, and so on. Let's invite all these guys to come and have a big kids' weekend.'

"So we did, and they came: basketball players Michael Jordan and Larry Bird, tennis players Jimmy Connors and John McEnroe, golfers Payne Stewart and Ray Floyd, entertainers Smokey Robinson and Woody Harrelson . . . and the Kenny Rogers Classic Weekend was born. The best athletes and entertainers in the world came to be kids again for the weekend. They competed in basketball, tennis, golf, and fishing, and at the end of it all we made enough money to build the Athens Area Homeless Shelter."

—*Kelly Junkermann*

Facing page: Kenny Rogers Classic Weekend, 1989. Participants included Larry Bird, Jimmy Connors, Michael Jordan, Alan Thicke, Woody Harrelson, and Smokey Robinson.
Courtesy of Kenny Rogers

SOURCES

Books

Butler, Larry, with Dave Goodenough. *Just for the Record: What It Takes to Make It in the Music Industry & in Life: Lessons from a Legend.* With a Foreword by Kenny Rogers. Pensacola, Florida: Indigo River Publishing, 2012.

Horstman, Dorothy. *Sing Your Heart Out, Country Boy.* 3rd ed. Nashville: Country Music Foundation Press, 1996.

Hume, Martha. *Kenny Rogers: Gambler, Dreamer, Lover.* Photographs by John Reggero. New York: New American Library, 1980.

Rogers, Kenny. *Luck or Something Like It.* New York: HarperCollins Publishers, 2012.

Interviews

Jimmy Bowen: April 30, 2014

Ken Kragen: March 20, 2014; March 26, 2014

Mary Miller: May 2, 2014

Jim Ed Norman: April 1, 2014

Billy Sherrill: April 7, 2014

Hat, jacket, and boots worn by Rogers in *The Gambler* TV movies.
Courtesy of Kenny Rogers / Photos by Bob Delevante

Correspondence

Bynum, Hal. "Writing Lucille." E-mail to John Rumble, April 1, 2014

Carnes, Kim. "Singing with Kenny." E-mail to John Rumble, March 27, 2014

Junkermann, Kelly. "Kenny Rogers Classic Weekend,"
"We Played Tons of Charity Events," and "We Were Kenny's Sherpas."
E-mail to John Rumble, May 5, 2014

McEntire, Reba. "I'm a Huge Kenny Rogers Fan."
E-mail to John Rumble, May 7, 2014

Parton, Dolly. Foreword. E-mail to Carolyn Tate,
April 30, 2014

Wheeler, Billy Edd. "Writing 'Coward of the County.'"
E-mail to John Rumble, March 19, 2014.

Video

Brooks, Garth. Remarks for Kenny Rogers's induction
into the Country Music Hall of Fame. October 27, 2013.

Below: Swingster windbreaker sold through Rogers's fan club, 1980s.
Courtesy of Kenny Rogers

Right: Souvenir mug from the
Dole-sponsored *Kenny Rogers
10th Anniversary Tour*, 1987.
*Courtesy of Sharman Pirkle
and Susan Bradley
Photo by Ryan Dooley*

Left: Promotional flying disc.
*Courtesy of Kirt Webster
Photo by Bob Delevante*

ACKNOWLEDGMENTS

This book and the exhibit it complements represent the contributions of many individuals and organizations. First, we are greatly indebted to Kenny Rogers for his generosity in sharing his extensive collection of memorabilia, and to his road manager, Gene Roy, who was primarily responsible for saving these treasures. We are also indebted to others on Rogers's team, especially Ken Levitan and Jason Henke, of Vector Management; Debbie Cross, of Kenny Rogers Productions; and Kirt Webster, of Webster & Associates, all of whom assisted greatly in assembling the book and exhibit.

In addition to writing the book's foreword, Dolly Parton loaned artifacts and images with help from her executive assistant, Teresa Hughes, and from Steve Summers, creative director of Dolly Parton Enterprises. Others who donated or loaned artifacts include Peggy Butler, Ron Harman, Kenny Rogers Productions creative director Kelly Junkermann, and Sharman Pirkle and Susan Bradley.

Ken Kragen, who managed Rogers for more than thirty years, not only shared materials from his personal collection, but also gave lengthy interviews that inform the exhibit and book alike. Producers Jimmy Bowen and Jim Ed Norman, First Edition vocalist Mary Miller, and recording engineer Billy Sherrill likewise contributed substantial interview time. At our request, Reba McEntire and singer-songwriters Hal Bynum, Kim Carnes, and Billy Edd Wheeler provided written accounts of their work with Rogers, as did Junkermann, who served as Rogers's tennis coach, doubles partner, and versatile project manager. We are also grateful to Teri Brown, of T.B.A. Network, Inc.; Andy Kerr, of Prime Source Entertainment Group; and Justin McIntosh, of Starstruck Entertainment, for their assistance in securing these interviews and revealing anecdotes.

Many museum staff members devoted time and talent to the exhibit and book. Space prohibits listing them all, but some deserve mention here. Vice President of Museum Services Carolyn Tate and project manager John Reed led the curatorial team, which consisted of principal curator Mick Buck; curators Tim Davis, Ryan Dooley, and Alan Stoker; and registrar Elek Horvath. Exhibits director Lee Rowe, creative director Warren Denney, lead designer Margaret Pesek, and exhibit designer Chris Doubler brought their skills to bear as well. John Rumble was principal writer and editor.

We are deeply grateful to SunTrust for its generous support of this exhibit. Likewise, we would like to thank the Metro Nashville Arts Commission and the Tennessee Arts Commission, both of which provide essential operating support that underwrites museum publications, school programs, and public programs.

Bronze bust of Kenny Rogers by Houston artist Eric Kaposta.
Courtesy of Ron Harman / Photo by Bob Delevante